UNDER THE CIRCUMSTANCES

Nikki Nikki
Under the Circumstances

All rights reserved
Copyright © 2023 by Nikki Nikki

No part of this publication may be reproduced, distributed, or transmitted in any form or by any means, including photocopying, recording, or other electronic or mechanical methods, without the prior written permission of the publisher, except in the case of brief quotations embodied in critical reviews and certain other noncommercial uses permitted by copyright law.

Published by BooxAi
ISBN: 978-965-578-400-8

UNDER THE CIRCUMSTANCES

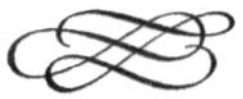

NIKKI NIKKI

THE TRAP

Baltimore City housing projects were a place with limited opportunities for growth and prosperity. One particular area was a community called Rodnell Heights, or The Heights, if you're from the neighborhood. The Heights was a community riddled with crime and violence. A place where danger lurked around every corner, and dreams seemed to wither away in the face of one obstacle after another. Within the narrow streets of The Heights, there were families who called this place home for generations. The hardships they faced were deeply ingrained as crime and poverty cast a dark shadow over their hopes and dreams.

It was in this place that Marcus was born. Marcus was tall, light-skinned, and handsome Marcus had a great sense of humor and a love for fashion. Marcus witnessed the struggles of his community firsthand; poverty, crime, and a lack of resources were a daily reality.

As Marcus grew older, he became increasingly aware of the limitations that his environment placed on him. He saw people around him resorting to illegal activities in the drug trade as a means of survival. The allure of quick money and the glamorous lifestyle that came with it began to tempt Marcus.

Feeling trapped and desperate for a way out of poverty, Marcus made the decision to enter the drug market. He saw it as a means to provide for his family and escape the hardships that surrounded him. It wasn't an easy choice, but he believed it was his only option at the time.

Marcus couldn't help but feel disillusioned by society's promises of success. He saw those around him succumbing to the temptations of quick money as an easy escape through illicit substances and decided to turn those vices into a means of liberation and success.

Soon, Marcus found himself immersed in a dangerous world, surrounded by violence, addiction, and money. He recruited a network of friends from his neighborhood by navigating the streets and making connections to further his trade. Soon after, the money started rolling in, and Marcus was living the life he had always envisioned.

He bought expensive cars, adorned himself in designer clothing, and lived in a lavish house. He traveled to luxurious destinations and met lots of people. He spared no expense for his family and friends. Marcus reveled in the material possessions and the sense of power that came with his newfound wealth, never giving a thought about the consequences.

Marcus was clever and resourceful. He had a keen understanding of the streets and knew how to navigate the hidden corners of his The Heights. He observed the patterns of the drug trade, the suppliers, the dealers, and the users. He studied the market and identified the loopholes that could be exploited to his advantage. Marcus believed that with the right connections and strategy, he could control a larger territory in Baltimore City and finally put an end to the poverty that had shackled his family for generations.

As the years passed by, Marcus became more determined to transform his dreams into reality. He knew that stepping further into the world of drug dealing came with immense risks,

but he was willing to take them. In his mind, the end justified the means. Marcus became a notorious figure with a reputation that preceded him. He demanded both respect and fear from those who crossed his path.

Along the way, he met a guy named Tony. Tony was a caramel complexion with an athletic build. A good-looking guy with a no-nonsense attitude. He was intelligent and a great dresser. Tony was a mysterious figure whose presence was felt but never seen. Both men were at the peak of their power, controlling the vast majority of the streets of Baltimore. The humble beginnings of the two men shaped their resilience and hunger for success. Their strategic minds, unparalleled audacity, and unwavering loyalty to their associates were also the foundation for a powerful friendship. The two recognized the qualities in each other that set them apart from the rest. A code of honor, invariable commitment to their people, and ruthless pragmatism. Embracing their newfound friendship, Marcus and Tony decided to merge their operations, creating an empire that would be unmatched in the criminal underworld. Their collaboration brought together Marcus's strategic brilliance and Tony's unmatched ability to navigate the streets undetected.

While navigating the dangerous streets of Baltimore, Marcus's path crosses with that of Janelle, a strong and independent woman who captures his attention. Janelle is a social worker dedicated to helping those affected by the violence and poverty rampant in the city, sees beyond Marcus's tough exterior, and recognizes the goodness within him.

Janelle is beautiful with rich ebony skin, brown eyes, and long wavy hair. She is tall and curvy with big breasts, a sharp mind, and a passion for entrepreneurship. She grew up in a middle-class neighborhood with two parents who instilled in her a strong work ethic and a sense of responsibility. As Marcus and Janelle spend more time together, their connection deepens. They discover shared values and a mutual desire to bring positive change to their community. Janelles's steady support and belief in Marcus' potential inspire him to redefine his priorities and seek a better life, not only for himself but also for those around him. Nervous but excited, Marcus decides to introduce Janelle to Tony, his right-hand man. It's the first time Marcus has ever declared that someone was special enough to be invited into his world. Janelle's presence immediately captivates Tony, who is not easily impressed by anyone. Her genuine kindness, intelligence, and immense support for Marcus leave a lasting impression on him. Tony sees how Janelle brings out the best in Marcus and recognizes her as a positive influence in Marcus's life.

Eager to embrace Janelle as a part of their tight-knit circle, Tony takes the initiative to introduce her to his wife and friends. He believes that Janelle's presence will not only enhance their friendships but also strengthen the sense of family they have cultivated over the years.

Nervous yet excited, Janelle meets Tony's wife, Maria, for the first time. Maria was a petite, vigorous, yet welcoming woman; she had a raspy voice with mocha skin, fine curves, and a keen sense for fashion. Maria built her strength through her adversities. Maria was emotionally resilient. She faced challenges head-on and never let setbacks discourage her. Maria led the wives and encouraged them to be strong for their men. She was the First Lady, and all the women in the group looked up to her. Maria immediately embraced Janelle, sensing the genuine love and respect she had for Tony and Marcus. Janelle's kindness and genuine nature instantly win Maria's approval, as she recognizes the positive impact Janelle has.

The friends, a diverse group with various backgrounds, warmly welcome Janelle into their fold. They value the two men's judgment and trust their choice to introduce Janelle as part of their family. Janelles' ability to connect with each of them on a personal level solidifies her place in their hearts, as they recognize her as a positive addition to their tight-knit group.

Janelle seamlessly integrates herself into the group, sharing laughs and stories and creating cherished memories with Tony's wife and friends. Her presence brings a fresh perspective and a sense of unity among everyone, fostering a deeper bond within the circle.

With Janelle officially embraced as part of the family. They come to see her as a pillar of support and love, just as they do Marcus. Together, they embark on a new chapter, solidifying their bonds and creating a united front against life's challenges.

The circle, now expanded to include Janelle, becomes a forever family. Janelle's acceptance into Marcus's inner circle not only strengthens their relationships but also creates a support system built on trust, love, and loyalty. They celebrate their unity and embrace the idea that family is not just tied by blood but by the connections and love they share. Maria plays a crucial role in supporting Janelle and helping her navigate her concerns about Marcus and his association with the streets as Janelle and Maria begin to get closer. They confide in one another about the pressures of their position. Maria is acclimated to her position. She encourages Janelle not to worry and shares stories about her life with Tony. Maria says that building a life with Tony wasn't easy. She revealed that throughout their relationship, Tony had been unfaithful, causing a great deal of pain and distrust between them. Despite this, Maria tried to work through their issues and remain committed to their partnership.

However, the ultimate blow came when Maria discovered that Tony had fathered a child with another woman while they were still together. This revelation shattered her, as she had always dreamed of having children but was unable to conceive. The fact that Tony had created a family with someone else while she struggled with infertility intensified her feelings of sadness and betrayal.

Ironically, it was during Tony's five-year stint in jail that they grew closer. Maria stood by his side, dedicating her life to him and offering him her total support. Her loyalty and love for Tony were unmatched, and she hoped that their bond would strengthen as they faced challenges together.

Eventually, Tony realized the depth of Maria's devotion and loyalty. As a result, he made the decision to marry her, understanding that she was the one person who had stood by him through thick and thin. Despite the hardships they faced, Maria believed that their love and commitment could overcome even the darkest moments.

Maria said that building a life with Tony had been far from easy, but Maria's dedication to their relationship showed her strength as a person. She hoped that, with time, they could heal the wounds caused by infidelity and build a stronger, more trusting future together.

Unbeknownst to Maria and despite difficult circumstances, Tony acknowledged that he hadn't fallen in love with Maria. However, he had a deep respect for her support and the sacrifices she had made during his time in jail.

Tony recognized that Maria had stood by him when many others would have walked away. He admired her strength and loyalty, which had helped him get through the toughest moments of his life. Maria had been his rock, providing emotional support and advocating for him throughout his incarceration.

While Tony couldn't force himself to feel romantic love for Maria, he knew that he owed her a debt of gratitude. He understood that she had put her own wants and needs aside to support him, and he felt a sense of responsibility to honor her commitment.

As they navigated their life together after Tony's release, he made a conscious effort to show his appreciation for Maria's role in his life. He treated her with kindness, respect, and the understanding that she deserved nothing less after all she had done for him.

Although their relationship may not have been founded on passionate love, Tony hoped that, over time, he could develop a deeper emotional connection with Maria. He recognized that love could grow and evolve, and he was willing to put in the effort to nurture their bond.

Tony's respect for Maria's support served as a foundation for their relationship. He believed that by fostering their friendship and building trust, their connection could potentially develop into a love that was based on more than just gratitude and respect.

Marcus had recently met with the family to discuss Janelle becoming a member. They all agreed that she was a good fit and that it was time. Maria was sent to talk to Janelle, so she invited Janelle out for lunch. She told Janelle not to bring her phone and gave her the time and location for the meeting. Once there, Janelle is greeted by Maria and then driven to another location. Janelle was nervous, but she was eager to spend time with Maria. She asked Janelle to be seated. Maria then began to speak, asking Janelle to relax as she started explaining the rules of her new underground family. Janelle listened intently as Maria began to speak, Marcus had explained many of the rules before she met with Maria, so she was prepared as Maria expressed that there were many expectations of Janelle and many rules Janelle was expected to follow. She was never to speak about anything she saw or knew about the family's activities to anyone outside the family. Janelle nodded, understanding the need for secrecy and the importance of trust within the family.

Maria continued, "We value loyalty above all else. You will be expected to support and protect your fellow family members at all costs. We have each other's backs no matter what." Janelle felt a sense of belonging wash over her as she listened to Maria's words. She had always longed for a strong support system, and it seemed like she had finally found it.

"Additionally," Maria added, "We operate on a strict code of conduct. Honesty and integrity are of utmost importance. We do not tolerate deceit or betrayal within this family. Trust is the foundation upon which we thrive."

Janelle nodded, realizing that being a part of this family meant she had to hold herself to a higher standard. She was determined to prove herself worthy and contribute to the family's success.

Maria then explained the family's mission and purpose.

"As a member of this family," Maria emphasized, "You will be expected to actively participate in our missions. We value intelligence, creativity, and resourcefulness. Each one of us brings unique skills to the table, and together, we make a formidable force."

Janelle's nervousness began to fade away, replaced by a sense of pride. She had always yearned for a purpose alongside her newfound family.

As Maria concluded her explanation, she looked at Janelle with a warm smile. "Remember, Janelle; we are here for you. We are a family in every sense of the word. If you ever need anything or have any questions, don't hesitate to ask."

Janelle felt a deep sense of gratitude towards Maria and the entire family. She knew that she had found a place where she truly belonged.

With renewed determination, Janelle took a deep breath and said, "I am ready to embrace this family, Maria."

Maria's eyes sparkled with pride as she replied, "Welcome." With that, Janelle officially became a member of her new family. Marcus was so proud. He knew that he had chosen the right woman to share his life with.

Janelle began being exposed to many different types of situations almost immediately. Janelle's experience in this unfamiliar territory constantly pushed the boundaries of her sanity. The sights she witnessed were far from what she anticipated; it was more than she could ever imagine, sparking a sense of outrage in her. Janelle had been thrust into an environment that she wasn't accustomed to. Janelle's journey into the unknown had taken an unexpected turn causing her agony and stress. The situations she found herself in were nothing short of bewildering.

What made matters worse was the feeling of being betrayed by Marcus, Tony, and Maria, who had presented the group as a family. As she began to understand her position in the family, she couldn't help but feel deceived. The realization that they had concealed the true nature of the family was agonizing. It was as if the ground beneath her had given way, leaving her to grapple with the confusion. In the midst of her anguish, Janelle had to find a way to navigate through this treacherous path alone. Janelle's situation was becoming increasingly difficult. The burden of her sworn allegiance to the family prevented her from confiding in anyone about her struggles. As a result, she felt incredibly lonely and miserable. The lack of emotional support started taking a toll on her mental well-being.

Sleep became a challenge for Janelle, and she found herself tossing and turning at night. During the day, feelings of paranoia consumed her, making it hard for her to focus or feel at ease. Janelle desperately needed someone to talk to, someone who could understand her predicament and offer advice.

In her desperation, she turned to Marcus, hoping he would empathize with her struggles. Janelle explained the reasons she felt unsafe and the nightmares she was experiencing. Unfortunately, Marcus had only known the life they were living, and to him, everything seemed great. He couldn't comprehend the depth of Janelle's distress, further isolating her in her pain.

Her concern deepens as she observes Marcus surrounded by a constant entourage of individuals who seem to orbit his world. She sees the danger lurking in the shadows; she's aware of the risk that comes along with Marcus in the drug trade. The streets are unforgiving and treacherous, but it has become his playground. Janelle fears that his sense of invincibility may lead to his demise.

Despite her worries, Janelle understands the allure that comes with Marcus' dangerous lifestyle. The power, the money, and the illusion of control can be intoxicating, making it difficult for him to see beyond the immediate gratification. She worries that Marcus has become desensitized to the harsh realities of the streets, blinded by the false sense of security that his position affords him.

Janelle longs for Marcus to recognize the risks he faces, to understand that his actions not only endanger himself but also those who care about him. She yearns for him to see the potential consequences of his choices, the lives that could be forever altered or lost in the wake of his involvement in the streets.

With every passing day, Janelle's concern for Marcus grows as she distances herself from the family, her heart heavy with the weight of the potential dangers that surround him. She hopes that one day he will awaken to the reality of his situation, to the fragility of life, and make a choice to distance himself from the streets that threaten to consume him. Janelle tries to steer him towards a safer and more legitimate path. She believes that encouraging him to open up a restaurant could provide him with a legitimate income and a sense of purpose. By challenging his skills and passion into a business venture, Marcus could not only distance himself from the dangers of the streets but could also have a positive impact on the community. Until then, she remains a steadfast presence in his life, a beacon of love and support, praying that her worries will not become a heartbreaking reality.

BUILDING A DREAM

*J*anelle and Marcus were working tirelessly to renovate the building in hopes of opening their first restaurant; they took on a huge project together but vowed to see it through. They wanted a place that would serve healthy and affordable food to the community. They were just a few months away from opening and were excited about the future. They talked about how life would be better once they opened the restaurant. They went on many trips in a quest to find new foods and culinary inspirations from around the country. These trips not only fueled their passion for food but also served as a reminder of the vast possibilities that lie ahead once their restaurant opens.

Janelle and Marcus's shared dream of opening a restaurant goes beyond just creating a successful business. It is also a way for Janelle to help Marcus leave his past life on the streets behind and embark on a new and fulfilling path.

As they work side by side in building their dream restaurant, Janelle and Marcus learn to rely on each other, trust each other's judgment, and overcome obstacles together. Janelle provides guidance, mentorship, and a safe space for Marcus to grow and thrive. Marcus, in turn, is inspired by Janelle's belief in him and pushes himself to prove her right.

Through their shared endeavor, Janelle and Marcus build a strong bond and sense of camaraderie. They celebrate each milestone achieved and learn from each setback. Together, they navigate the challenges of starting a business, all the while keeping their eyes on the ultimate goal of creating a place that will not only serve healthy and affordable food but also provide an opportunity for Marcus to leave the streets behind for good, It is a testament to their resilience, determination, and the power of a shared vision. Tony plays a crucial role in their journey towards building their dream restaurant. Tony recognizes the potential in both Janelle and Marcus and is determined to support them in any way he can.

As an experienced entrepreneur, Tony offers valuable insights and guidance to Marcus and Janelle. He shares his knowledge of the industry, helps them with business planning, and assists in navigating the complexities of starting a restaurant. Tony's expertise and Marias' advice become invaluable resources for Janelle and Marcus as they navigate the challenges of building their business.

Furthermore, Tony uses his network and connections to open doors for Janelle and Marcus. He introduces them to potential investors, suppliers, and other key players in the restaurant industry. Through his extensive contacts, Tony helps Janelle and Marcus secure partnerships and gain access to resources that would have otherwise been inaccessible to them.

Beyond the professional aspect, Tony and Maria also serve as mentors and a source of emotional support for Marcus. They understand the difficulties Marcus has faced and offer guidance on personal development, stability, and overcoming adversity. Their belief in Marcus's potential serves as a constant reminder that he can truly create a brighter future for himself.

The support and encouragement motivate them to keep pushing forward, even when faced with setbacks and challenges.

Together, Janelle, Marcus, Tony, and Maria form a close-knit support system, united by their shared goal of building the dream restaurant. With Tony's guidance and assistance, Janelle and Marcus have a stronger foundation to turn their dream into a reality and create a lasting impact on their lives and the community they serve.

A TRAGIC LOSS

One morning, Janelle woke up to a panicked phone call. Marcus had been shot in the streets of Baltimore City. She rushed to the hospital, praying that he would pull through, but it was not meant to be. Marcus passed away, leaving Janelle devastated and alone. The sudden death of Marcus was a blow that I never expected. We had been so happy together, planning our future and dreaming of all the things we wanted to do. But then, in the blink of an eye, everything changed.

The days that followed were a blur. Janelle couldn't eat or sleep, and she felt like a part of me had died with him. She couldn't imagine a life without him, and the thought of never seeing him again was too much to bear. Grief enveloped Janelle like a suffocating fog. The loss of her beloved Marcus was an indescribable pain that pierced her heart and soul. She felt not only devastated but also utterly alone. Their dreams together, their plans for the future, all shattered in an instant. Days turned into nights, and Janelle's sorrow became her constant companion. The world seemed to move forward, oblivious to her pain. However, amidst the darkness, Janelle found moments of solace in memories of Marcus. She cherished every laugh, every touch, every shared secret they had.

They had always talked about how much they loved each other, but she never realized just how much until he was gone. Every moment spent together was precious, and she wished she had taken more time to appreciate it all.

The funeral was far too painful for Janelle to attend. She saw his family and friends grieving, but it all felt surreal. It wasn't until she saw his lifeless body in the casket online that it really hit her. He was gone, and there was nothing she could do to bring him back.

Janelle was in a state of shock and disbelief. She had lost the love of her life, the person she had built a future with. She felt like she had no one to turn to and spent hours sitting in the dark, trying to make it through the pain. As the weeks and months went by, she struggled to come to terms with his death. She missed him every day, and everything reminded her of him. She'd see something funny and think, "I have to tell him about this," only to realize that he wasn't there to share it with. Never did she imagine what loneliness and vulnerability could do. She had no idea of just what was to come. In the depths of solitude, her soul began to wither, consumed by an overwhelming sense of emptiness. The once vibrant colors of life faded into shades of gray, leaving her lost in a desolate landscape. Each passing day felt like a slow descent into a bottomless abyss as she grappled with the weight of her own isolation.

The world around her seemed to carry on, oblivious to Janelle's silent suffering. Friends and family became distant figures, their presence reduced to mere memories. The laughter and warmth that once filled her days became distant echoes, haunting reminders of a time when connection and belonging were within reach.

Vulnerability became Janelle's constant companion, an unwelcome guest that stripped away the protective layers she had carefully constructed. Janelle found herself exposed, raw, and defenseless against the harsh realities of life. Every interaction became a reminder of her own fragility as she yearned for understanding and acceptance.

As the days turned into weeks and weeks into months, Janelle began to question her worth. Doubts and insecurities gnawed at the edges of her consciousness, eroding the confidence she once held. She felt like she was nothing without Marcus. It was hard to remember what life was like before him. She struggled to find meaning or purpose in her existence. Every day felt like a battle as she faced the overwhelming emptiness and grief that consumed her. Never did she imagine that grief and sadness could lead her on such a long journey of vulnerability and loneliness. Through the depths of despair, she became weaker and more confused.

One day, when Janelle was at her lowest point, she received a phone call from Tony. Tony, a close friend of

Marcus and Janelle, had heard about her struggles and wanted to reach out and offer his support. Little did Janelle know that this phone call would become a lifeline for her.

As they began to talk, Tony listened patiently and empathetically to Janelle's pain. He didn't try to minimize her feelings or offer quick fixes. Instead, he simply held space for her to express her emotions and validated her grief. His presence on the other end of the line provided a sense of comfort and peace that Janelle desperately needed.

For hours, Tony patiently stayed on the phone with Janelle, allowing her to pour out her heartache and sorrow. He shared stories about Marcus, reminiscing about the joyous times they had all spent together. Through his words, Tony painted a vivid picture of Marcus's vibrant spirit and the impact he had on those around him.

Tony's compassion and understanding helped Janelle realize that her life did have meaning, even without Marcus. He reminded her of the love they had shared and the memories they had created together. He encouraged her to hold onto those memories and find ways to honor Marcus's legacy.

Furthermore, Tony encouraged Janelle to continue working on the restaurant. He assured her that he would continue to support her with the project. He reminded her that she was not alone in her pain and that he cared for her and wanted to help her through this difficult time.

With Tony's support and guidance, Janelle began the process of completing the restaurant that she and Marcus had always dreamed of. The restaurant had been their shared passion, and Janelle saw it as a way to honor Marcus's memory while also finding a new purpose for herself.

Tony played a crucial role in helping Janelle navigate the challenges of starting a business. He connected her with experienced restaurateurs who could offer advice and guidance. He helped finalize all the details. Tony's belief in Janelle's abilities and his constant encouragement gave her the confidence to move forward with her plans.

As Janelle threw herself into the restaurant project, she found a renewed sense of purpose and direction. The process of designing the menu, hiring staff, and creating a welcoming atmosphere became a therapeutic outlet for her grief. Each step forward brought a glimmer of hope and a reminder that she was capable of building a life beyond her pain.

Throughout the journey, Tony remained by Janelle's side, offering support and practical assistance whenever she needed it. He was there for late-night brainstorming sessions, helping her fine-tune the menu and make important decisions. He pitched in with physical labor, helping with renovations and setting up the space. Tony's dedication and selflessness were a constant reminder that Janelle was not alone in her endeavors.

Finally, the day came when Janelle opened the doors of the restaurant. It was a bittersweet moment, as she felt the absence of Marcus keenly. But as she looked around at the bustling space, filled with happy customers enjoying their meals, she knew that she had created something beautiful out of her pain.

The restaurant became a gathering place for friends, family, and the local community. Janelle poured her heart and soul into creating an atmosphere that reflected Marcus's spirit and the love they had shared. It became a place where people could come together, enjoy delicious food, and cherish the memories of those they had lost.

Janelle's journey from hitting rock bottom to opening the restaurant was filled with moments of doubt and grief. But through Tony's constant support, she found the strength to persevere and turn her passion into a reality. The restaurant became a symbol of love and healing not only for Janelle but also a testament to the power of friendship and the ability to find purpose and joy even in the face of devastating loss.

As Janelle continued to run the restaurant, she always carried Marcus's memory in her heart. Each day, she found comfort in knowing that she was living a life that he would be proud of, and in those moments when the grief threatened to overwhelm her, she would call Tony, his words of encouragement and the journey they had embarked on together reminded her that she was never alone.

Over time, Janelle learned to navigate her grief and find purpose in her life once again. She realized that while Marcus's death had left a void in her heart, she still had the power to create a meaningful life for herself. Through the restaurant and Tony's ongoing friendship, Janelle begins to rebuild her life and find joy in small moments.

The phone call from Tony became a turning point for Janelle. It reminded her that even in the darkest times, there are people who care and are willing to offer support. It taught her that it's okay to lean on others during difficult times and that healing is possible, even in the face of devastating loss.

A NEW CONNECTION

Janelle and Tony started talking more and more, finding comfort in each other's company. They'd talk for hours, and she felt like she was getting to know him on a deeper level. They shared things they'd never told anyone. They had both lost someone they loved and understood the pain of grief. They built a strong friendship that soon began to depend on each other to get through the pain. As Janelle and Tony opened up to each other about their pasts and their shared experiences of loss, their friendship deepened. They found comfort in each other's understanding and empathy, knowing that they were not alone in their grief. They became each other's pillars of support, providing compassion and strength during the darkest moments.

In their conversations, Janelle and Tony discovered a profound connection that went beyond their shared pain. They shared their dreams, fears, and hopes for the future.

They found happiness in each other's presence, often seeking refuge in their conversations to escape the weight of their grief. Janelle listened attentively as Tony poured his heart out about his loveless marriage. He spoke of the emotional distance between him and his wife and how their lack of intimacy had taken a toll on their relationship. Tony revealed that he had been sleeping on the sofa for over a year, unable to find love in their shared bed.

Tony's words painted a picture of a crumbling connection, where the spark that once ignited their love had long since faded away. Janelle could sense the pain in his voice, the longing for something more, and the desperation to find happiness again.

As Tony continued to open up, Janelle offered him a compassionate ear, providing comfort and support. She encouraged him to communicate with his wife and to express his feelings and desires honestly. Janelle acknowledged that navigating such difficult conversations could be challenging but emphasized the importance of addressing their issues head-on.

Janelle reminded Tony that love and relationships require effort from both parties.

Throughout their conversation, Janelle remained empathetic, understanding the weight of Tony's confession. She assured him that his words were safe with her and that he was not alone; she explained to him that many couples faced similar challenges. Janelle reminded him that love and relationships often go through ups and downs and that with effort, understanding, and open communication, they had a chance to rebuild or recreate their relationship. Tony felt a sense of relief and gratitude for Janelle's support.

Janelle resented that Tony was being treated so poorly in his marriage. She hated seeing him trudge through his deteriorating relationship. It pained her to witness the abuse. The anger and frustration she felt towards his wife, Maria, was palpable. She couldn't understand why Tony tolerated such treatment. The irritation consumed her, clouding her judgment and preventing her from seeing the full picture. Janelle was so angry that Tony was being treated badly that she began to have conversations with her friends, who offered a different perspective. They suggested that Maria felt that Tony was unavailable and inconsistent, but she knew that he was a good man and that what they were saying was false. Janelle felt that she was the only one that really understood him.

As time went on, Janelle began to realize that her feelings for Tony were evolving beyond friendship. She found herself longing for his presence and cherishing their time together. The thought of Tony became a source of joy and comfort, a beacon of light amidst the darkness.

Afraid to risk their friendship, Janelle hesitated to express her feelings to Tony. She feared that it might complicate their relationship or lead to rejection. Especially since he was married, but the more they leaned on each other, the stronger her feelings grew, and she couldn't deny the depth of her emotions any longer. Janelle felt that she and Tony were both great people who deserved to be happy.

One evening, as they sat together in the quiet of the restaurant after closing, Janelle mustered up the courage to share her feelings with Tony. With a mix of nervousness and vulnerability, she poured her heart out, expressing how much he meant to her and how she had come to see him as more than just a friend. She explained the sadness she felt for him and described how she felt he deserved someone who loved him.

To her surprise, Tony's reaction was one of understanding and reciprocation. He revealed that he had been grappling with similar feelings and that their connection had become something he cherished deeply. They both acknowledged the complexity of their situation but agreed to explore their newfound romantic feelings together, taking it one step at a time. Tony leaned over and kissed Janelle on her lips. At that moment, she had forgotten that he was married. Her mind was clouded with desire and perplexity. She couldn't resist the pull she felt towards him. The kiss was so passionate and intense that it ignited a fire within Janelle that she hadn't felt since Marcus. Tony and Janelle knew that they had to make love; the burning attraction between them made it inevitable. Tony quickly began to undress Janelle; he had been longing to feel her body for months, and the opportunity had finally come. Tony was pleased from the moment he entered her body. Her pussy was perfect. It was soft, hot, and creamy. It was everything he had hoped for; he took his time as their bodies became one. Tony pushed his big dick back and forth inside Janelle's wet pussy. Janelle loved the feeling she got as he pushed himself deeper into her body. They both enjoyed the intensity of each stroke as they moved in slow motion on one accord giving into their yearning for each other. As they rose to ecstasy, they embraced each other's bodies tightly and let their desires consume them. Their hands explored every curve and crevice, their lips locked in a passionate dance. Sweat trickled down their heated skin, fueling the fire that burned within them. Their hearts beat in synchrony, pounding with the intensity of their shared pleasure.

Moans and whispers filled the air, mingling with the sounds of their fervent lovemaking. Time seemed to stand still as their bodies moved in synchrony, lost in a world of their own creation. Each touch, each kiss, sent waves of pleasure crashing through them, heightening their connection and pushing them closer to the edge of bliss.

At that moment, nothing else mattered. They were consumed by the raw intensity of their desire, surrendering themselves to the overwhelming power that coursed through their veins. Every touch was electric, every breath a desperate gasp for more.

As they reached the pinnacle of their passion, their bodies trembled with the intensity of their release. Waves of pleasure washed over them, leaving them breathless and sated. In the aftermath, they held each other close, their bodies intertwined, basking in the afterglow of their shared ecstasy.

At that moment, they knew they had experienced something transcendental, a connection that went beyond the physical. It was a moment of pure intimacy, where their souls merged, and their bodies became one. And as they lay there, wrapped in each other's arms, they knew that this was just the beginning, and they were not going to stop even though Tony was married. They had now crossed the line and were fully immersed in the depths of their newfound passion. The boundaries that once defined their relationship had blurred. They found themselves craving more and more of each other's touch, more of each other's love.

With each passing day their connection grew stronger and deeper. They couldn't resist the magnetic pull that drew them together, igniting a flame that refused to be extinguished. They found peace in each other's presence, their souls intertwining in a dance only they could understand. Their conversations flowed effortlessly, words becoming mere vessels for the emotions they shared. Time seemed to stand still whenever they were together as if the universe conspired to create a space solely for their love.

Every touch, every glance, sent electric currents through their bodies, awakening a deep desire that burned within. Their connection was more than physical; it was a meeting of minds, a meeting of hearts. They understood each other on a level no one else could, communicating without uttering a single word.

In each other's arms, they found strength, comfort, and acceptance. They became each other's sanctuary, a safe haven amidst a chaotic world. Their love was a force that could weather any storm, for it was built on a foundation of trust, vulnerability, and unwavering support.

Together, they explored the depths of their beings, unearthing hidden parts of themselves they never knew existed. They challenged each other to grow, to evolve, to become the best versions of themselves. With gentle guidance, they healed each other's wounds and embraced every flaw, knowing that it was their imperfections that made them perfect for one another.

They cherished the little moments, the stolen glances, the stolen kisses like treasures. And in the grander moments, they celebrated their love, their hearts overflowing with gratitude for finding each other in a vast sea of possibilities.

But as their love grew, so did their fear of losing it. They knew that love was a delicate balance, and they were both aware of the fragility of their connection due to the circumstances that threatened their relationship. Yet, they refused to let fear dictate their actions. Instead, they chose to hold on tighter, to fight for what they believed in.

Their flame burned brighter with every obstacle they overcame, every hurdle they leaped together. It was a flame that refused to be extinguished, a love that defied all odds.

They nurtured their love, cherishing the gift they had found in one another. For they knew that true love, the kind that defies logic and transcends time, was a rare and precious gem, and they were determined to treasure it for as long as they could.

They explored uncharted territories, discovering hidden depths of pleasure and intimacy they had never experienced before. Their passion knew no boundaries, and they relished in the freedom they found in each other's embrace.

Janelle thought about Tony constantly. She knew that she was in over her head, but she didn't mind. The pleasure was greater than the pain at that moment, and she enjoyed it. She only wished she'd met Tony first before meeting Marcus.

Tony was different from Marcus in many ways. His gentle and mature nature was captivating.

While Marcus was outgoing and charismatic, Tony possessed a calm and reserved demeanor. He had a way of carrying himself that exuded tranquility and wisdom beyond his years. Tony treated Janelle to a wonderful time, showering her with exquisite jewelry, stylish clothes, trendy shoes, generous amounts of money, and delicious food. They explored enchanting destinations together. Tony was always considerate and kind, taking the time to listen and understand Janelle's perspectives. He was always considerate and kind, taking the time to listen and understand people's perspectives. His patience and empathy made him a great listener and a trusted confidant.

His genuine concern for her well-being reminded her of the love and care she had lost. He listened to her without judgment, offering a shoulder to lean on and a comforting touch when words failed her. He became her safe space, a source of strength and comfort during her darkest moments.

A COMPLICATED RELATIONSHIP

Janelle and Tony's relationship was complicated. He was Marcus' best friend, and he was also married. Janelle felt guilty about her feelings for him but couldn't deny the attraction they shared. She knew that Marcus would want her to be happy and that Tony was a good person, but their relationship would cause controversy, especially from Tony's wife, who would feel betrayed.

Due to her past experiences with Tony, Maria suspected the affair. She felt the chemistry between the two of them. She forbids Janelle from coming around again.

Tony's decision to continue the affair while still living with his wife created a multitude of problems in their relationship. The constant deceit and betrayal eroded the trust between Tony and Janelle, making it difficult for them to communicate and find common ground;

however, Janelle was determined to make it work, so she decided to support his decision to stay with his wife.

Tony's wife started to notice changes in his behavior as well, such as being more distant and secretive. She became suspicious and confronted him about her concerns. However, Tony continued to deny any wrongdoing and insisted that everything was fine.

The tension and strain in their relationship grew as Maria began to become suspicious. One day while Tony was in the shower, Maria went through his phone and was able to uncover evidence of the affair. She found a message from Janelle, leaving her devastated and hurt.

As Maria's emotions ran high, she couldn't resist the urge to confront Janelle directly. She dialed Janelle's number, her hand trembling with a mix of anger, hurt, and desperation. After a few rings, Janelle picked up the phone, her voice revealing surprise and unease.

"Janelle, it's Maria," she said, her voice quivering. "I found the messages between you and my husband. How could you do this to me?"

There was a momentary silence on the other end of the line before Janelle responded, her voice filled with remorse. "Maria, I am so sorry. I never meant for any of this to happen. It was a mistake, and I deeply regret it. I didn't mean to send that message to your husband; there's nothing going on between us!!"

Maria's anger flared up as she thought about the betrayal. "A mistake? How can you call it a mistake? You knew he was married, Janelle. You knew what you were doing."

Janelle's voice softened, carrying a hint of tears. "I explained why it happened, Maria. It's not an excuse; I have multiple Tonys in my contacts!! I sent the message to the wrong Tony!! "I never intended to hurt you." I apologize!

Torn between rage and the desire to understand, Maria took a deep breath, attempting to calm herself. "I don't know if I can ever forgive you, Janelle. You've shattered my trust and my marriage."

Janelle's voice wavered. "I understand, Maria. I truly do. All I can ask for is your forgiveness and the chance to make amends in any way possible. I never wanted to cause you this much pain." The message was sent to the wrong number.

Maria paused, "Janelle, I can't promise forgiveness right now until I know the truth, but I want you to understand the gravity of your actions," Maria said, her voice filled with a mix of sadness and determination. "This affair has deeply wounded me, and if it's true, you will pay the consequences. For now, "You are no longer in the family; I need space to process everything." You are not to come back around, my husband!

Janelle sighed, acknowledging Maria's request. "I respect that, Maria. I am truly sorry for the pain I've caused. If there's anything I can do to make things right, please let me know."

Maria ended the call, feeling a sense of relief mixed with lingering pain. When Tony returned from the shower, Maria confronted him. She told him that she had contacted Janelle and insisted that the affair end immediately. As Maria argued, all he could think about was Janelle; the thought of losing her devastated him. Tony's heart sank as he absorbed the gravity of the situation. He knew he had caused immense pain to both Janelle and his wife, Maria. Overwhelmed with guilt, he realized that he needed to face the consequences of his actions and be there for Janelle in her time of need.

Without wasting a moment, Tony gathered his thoughts, determined to offer Janelle the support she deserved. He rushed to Janelle's place, his mind racing with apologies and a sincere desire to make things right.

As Tony arrived at Janelle's doorstep, he took a deep breath to calm his nerves. He knocked gently, feeling a mix of anxiety and anticipation. Janelle opened the door, her eyes weary from tears, but upon seeing Tony, a wave of conflicting emotions washed over her face.

"Janelle," Tony began, his voice filled with remorse, "I am so sorry for the pain I've caused you. There are no excuses for my actions, and I understand if you can't forgive me. But please know that I am here to listen, to support you, and to do whatever I can to help you heal."

Janelle's eyes brimmed with tears once again, but she appreciated Tony's willingness to face the consequences and his genuine concern. She invited him inside, signaling that she was open to hearing what he had to say.

Sitting down together, Tony and Janelle engaged in a heartfelt conversation. Tony listened attentively as Janelle poured out her feelings of betrayal, sadness, and confusion. She acknowledged the pain she had caused his wife devastated her, and she wanted to end the affair. Tony spoke, also taking responsibility for his actions and ensuring Janelle that he deeply regretted hurting them both. Tony told Janelle that there was no way he could let her go; he told her that he was in love with her and that he just needed some time to make things right.

With empathy and compassion, Tony shared his own struggle with the situation, expressing his remorse and the immense guilt he felt about being married and best friends with Marcus. He said he knew that the relationship would be difficult, but he wanted to continue with the journey. Tony said that this was the first time he had ever truly been happy in a relationship. He acknowledged the need for making amends not only to Janelle but also to his wife, Maria, for the affair but assured Janelle that he was leaving Maria soon.

"I understand if you need time and space, Janelle," Tony said sincerely. "But please know that I am committed to making things right and making every effort to rebuild trust and repair the damage I've caused."

Janelle, though still devastated, saw the sincerity in Tony's eyes and the genuine remorse he displayed. She appreciated his willingness to confront the situation head-on and his commitment to her well-being.

"Tony," Janelle replied, her voice filled with a mixture of sadness and cautious hope, "I can't deny the pain I feel right now, but I'm in love with you too." I'm not going anywhere, Janelle stated.

Tony nodded, grateful for Janelle's willingness to consider a path forward. "Thank you, Janelle," he said earnestly. "I know we have a long road ahead, but with your patience and understanding, I truly believe we can navigate through this and emerge stronger individuals."

In the days that followed, Maria forbids the ladies of the family from having any contact with Janelle, confiding in them about the affair and the pain she was experiencing. They offered her empathy, understanding, and guidance, reminding her that she was not alone in this difficult journey.

As time passed, Tony's wife, Maria, felt a deepening sense of resentment and anger towards him. The realization that Tony was continuing the affair despite knowing the pain it caused her left her feeling betrayed and disrespected. She couldn't fathom why he would choose to hurt her in such a way, especially since she had been so loyal and committed to him and the marriage.

Maria's emotions were a mixture of confusion, sadness, and anger. She struggled to comprehend the reasons behind Tony's actions, desperately searching for answers that would provide clarity and make sense of the situation. The more she dwelled on it, the more her bafflement grew.

She confronted Tony, demanding an explanation for his behavior. Maria questioned his commitment to their marriage and the trust they had built over the years. She expressed her deep hurt and asked him why he would continue the affair despite the damage it inflicted upon her and their relationship.

Tony, feeling overwhelmed and guilty, struggled to find the right words to explain himself. He denied his love for the other woman, Janelle, but acknowledged that he was torn between his feelings for her and his commitment to his marriage.

Maria hurt and frustrated, found it difficult to accept Tony's explanation. She couldn't comprehend how she could easily give up on the marriage. The sense of betrayal weighed heavily on her, leaving her feeling lost and deceived.

The ensuing days and weeks were filled with tension and emotional turmoil. Maria grappled with the conflicting emotions of love, anger, and sadness. She contemplated the future of their marriage and wondered if forgiveness and healing were even possible.

Tony, realizing the extent of the damage he had caused, made efforts to communicate openly with Maria. He listened to her frustrations, acknowledged her pain, and expressed his remorse for the hurt he had inflicted. He assured her that he wanted to find a solution that would bring them both peace and happiness.

Over time, Tony tries harder to please Maria but arguments and fights become a regular occurrence in their household. The emotional turmoil took a toll on both Tony and Maria, causing them immense pain and suffering. The toxic atmosphere affected their mental and emotional well-being, leaving them both feeling trapped and unhappy.

Tony's lack of understanding regarding Maria's anger and resentment only further strained their relationship. He failed to grasp the depth of her pain and the reasons behind her emotional turmoil. Instead, he justified his actions and minimized the significance of his affair.

In his perspective, Tony believed he had successfully hidden the affair from Maria, which led him to question why she was so angry. He felt a sense of accomplishment for having kept the affair a secret, unaware of the toll it had taken on Maria's emotions.

Furthermore, Tony's belief that Maria should be grateful for the life he had provided her only added insult to injury. His dismissive attitude towards Maria's feelings deepened her sense of betrayal and resentment.

Tony's inability to comprehend Maria's anger also stemmed from his own emotional detachment from her. He admitted to Maria that he'd never fallen in love with her, which further undermined their relationship. This revelation only intensified Maria's feelings of hurt and betrayal, as it exposed the lack of emotional investment Tony had in their marriage.

Despite the turmoil, Tony was unable to end the affair and face the consequences of his actions. He was torn between his feelings for Janelle and his commitment to his wife. This indecisiveness only added to the chaos in their relationship, leaving everyone involved in a state of constant turmoil.

Tony and Janelle were spending time together every day. The affair became unbearable for Janelle as well. She had initially been drawn to the excitement and passion of their forbidden relationship, but as time went on, Janelle started to feel the weight of guilt and shame creeping in. The secrecy and lies began to take a toll on her emotional well-being, and she found herself constantly anxious and on edge.

Janelle had always prided herself on being an honest and trustworthy person, but this affair had made her question her own integrity. She knew that she was betraying her own values and the commitment she had made to herself. The guilt ate away at her conscience, causing her sleepless nights and a constant feeling of unease.

Tony refused to leave his home, where he had many responsibilities, but Janelle couldn't continue living in secrecy and guilt. The affair had been going on for two years now.

Despite Janelle's initial intention to end the affair, Tony persisted in convincing her to stay. He played on her emotions, reminding her of the intense passion and excitement they shared. Tony assured Janelle that their love was worth fighting for and that they could find a way to make it work.

Janelle found herself torn between her desire for a stable, faithful relationship and her strong feelings for Tony. She knew deep down that continuing the affair would only lead to more pain and turmoil, but Tony's persuasive words and promises of a future together clouded her judgment.

Janelle started noticing patterns in Tony's behavior that made her question his intentions. He would often say one thing but do another, leaving her feeling confused and hurt. It seemed like he enjoyed playing with her emotions, manipulating her to get what he wanted.

For instance, Tony would often make promises that he couldn't keep. He would say he would change his ways or prioritize their relationship, only to fall back into his old habits shortly after. Janelle's heart ached every time Tony would shower her with affection, only to abruptly walk away without a second thought. It was a constant cycle of hope and disappointment that left her feeling confused and hurt.

She couldn't understand why Tony would invest so much time and effort into their relationship only to vanish without any explanation. It was as if he enjoyed the thrill of pursuing her but had no interest in committing or building something substantial.

The emotional roller coaster was exhausting for Janelle. She yearned for stability and a genuine relationship, but Tony seemed incapable of providing that. She questioned whether there was something wrong with her or if she simply wasn't enough to keep him interested.

As time went on, Janelle's resentment grew. She began to hate Tony for playing with her emotions and using her as a temporary source of affection.

Deep down, Janelle knew she needed to break free from this toxic cycle. She couldn't continue subjecting herself to the pain of watching Tony love her one moment only to leave her heartbroken the next.

This inconsistency left Janelle feeling unimportant and insignificant in his life. Janelle was in shock. This wasn't the man she fell in love with. The disappointment of this relationship was too much to bear. Janelle's trust in Tony again began to fade. She found herself constantly in doubt, wondering if he was being honest with her. She wondered if he would really leave his wife and provide the life he'd promised her. The emotional roller coaster became exhausting. Janelle knew she deserved better than someone she had to share.

Finally, the strain between the two women became unbearable.

The constant arguments between Tony and Janelle about his tendency to leave had become a regular occurrence in their relationship. Janelle's frustration with his inconsistency and inability to commit had reached a breaking point.

Meanwhile, Tony's marriage with Maria had also brought its fair share of problems. The constant arguments between him and Maria about him staying in the affair were wearing him down. He felt torn between his feelings for Maria and the excitement he found in his affair with Janelle.

The toll of juggling these two relationships was starting to weigh heavily on Tony. He couldn't deny the emotional strain it caused him to constantly switch between the two women, trying to please them both while maintaining his own happiness.

Tony knew he had to make a decision, not only for his own well-being but also for the sake of the women involved. The constant arguments and emotional turmoil were no longer sustainable, and he needed to choose a path that would bring clarity and peace.

As hard as it was, Tony realized that he couldn't continue hurting both Janelle and Maria any longer.

Tony made the difficult decision to separate from his wife. It was undoubtedly a hard thing for him to do, but the affair had caused irreparable damage to his marriage because he had fallen in love with Janelle.

STARTING OVER

Janelle was excited about Tony's decision, and she was determined to make the most of every moment, cherishing their love. She was forever grateful for the chance to start fresh and create a life that they would be proud of. She wanted Tony to know that he had made the right decision. She was elated that he'd finally left his wife to be with her. She was so happy to finally be chosen by Tony. It was the moment she dreamt about. Tony had ultimately decided to be with her!! All of her patience had paid off. She soon found herself daydreaming about becoming Mrs. Tony Ceasar, but he hadn't divorced Maria yet, so she didn't want to get too carried away, especially since Maria called on Tony for everything. This was unsettling to Janelle.

Janelle's heart was filled with a mixture of excitement and apprehension. While she was thrilled that Tony had chosen to be with her, the fact that he hadn't finalized his divorce from Maria weighed on her mind. She understood that divorces could be complex and time-consuming, but the constant presence of Maria in Tony's life unsettled her.

Despite her concerns, Janelle remained determined to make their relationship work. She knew that true love required patience and understanding, so she decided to focus on building a strong foundation with Tony. She reassured herself that their love was worth the wait, and that eventually, they would overcome these obstacles together.

Janelle made it a priority to communicate openly and honestly with Tony about her feelings. She wanted him to know that while she was overjoyed to be chosen by him, the lingering presence of Maria in their lives made her feel uneasy. Together, they discussed how they could navigate this situation with respect and consideration for all parties involved.

In the meantime, the two continued to cherish every moment they spent together. They explored beautiful places, enjoying romantic dinners and creating memories that would last a lifetime. Janelle's creativity and smart thinking allowed her to come up with unique date ideas that brought them closer together.

She also supported Tony through the challenges he faced with Maria. Janelle understood that it was not easy for him to sever ties completely, and she offered her assistance in any way she could. Whether it was helping him organize his affairs or providing emotional support, Janelle was there for Tony every step of the way.

As time went on, Janelle's friendly and caring nature helped create a strong bond between them. She remained hopeful that one day, she would become Mrs. Tony Ceasar, but she knew that their love was more than just a title. Their journey together was about building a life of happiness and fulfillment, and Janelle was committed to making that dream a reality

FACING THE PAST

anelle couldn't understand why Tony was still so involved with Maria despite their new life together. It seemed like every time Maria needed something, she would call on Tony for help, and he would always go running. Janelle felt like she was constantly competing for Tony's attention and affection, and it was causing a strain on their relationship. Tony seemed to be spending lots of time fixing up and repairing the house he swore he hated. Suddenly he was always at Maria's place. Janelle was completely clueless about why he cared so much right now, as they had just started their new life together.

Tony, on the other hand, felt a deep sense of gratitude towards Maria. She had been there for him during his darkest times, providing support and care when he needed it the most. He couldn't shake off the feeling that he owed her, and it made him feel obligated to always be there for her.

This dynamic created tension between Tony and Janelle. Janelle couldn't understand why Tony couldn't set boundaries with Maria and prioritize their relationship. She felt like she was always playing second fiddle to Maria's needs, and it made her question whether Tony truly valued their relationship.

Conversations about the issue often turned into arguments, with Janelle expressing her frustration with Maria's dependency and Tony feeling torn between his loyalty to Maria and his love for Janelle. It seemed like an impossible situation, and both of them were growing tired of the constant conflict.

As time went on, the calls from Maria became more frequent. She discovered the immense power she had over Tony, and she couldn't resist having a little fun with it, especially knowing how much it upset Janelle. She would call him all hours of the day, sometimes in the middle of the night, pretending to be in dire need of assistance, and every single time Tony would answer her call and rush to her aid. Janelle knew that Maria was playing games.

She needed Tony to understand how his actions were affecting their relationship and make a decision about where his loyalty truly lay.

Tony had always been a stand-up guy, and this trait had led him down a path of constantly catering to Maria's every need. He had never ended a relationship before, so he didn't know how to assert himself or set boundaries.

Maria, aware of this, took advantage of Tony's willingness to do anything for her.

Maria continued to exploit Tony's loyalty. She would make up ridiculous stories about her car breaking down or her basement flooding. Maria called on Tony for money, repairs, hauling away items, etc… just about anything she could think of, and Tony would rush to her side, leaving Janelle feeling more frustrated.

One evening after rushing to Maria's house to "fix a leaking roof," Tony returned home to find Janelle waiting for him, visibly upset. Janelle couldn't hold back her emotions any longer and confronted him about the constant availability for Maria.

"Why do you always drop everything and run to her when she calls?" Janelle asked, her voice cracking, filled with hurt and frustration.

Tony took a deep breath, reaching out to hold Janelle's trembling hands, and replied, "Because she is my wife," his voice filled with a mixture of love and regret. Janelle felt as if her whole world was crushed in the blink of an eye. Tears streamed down her face. Janelle replied, "Then why are you here?" Tony sensing the depth of Janelle's pain, gently cupped her face in his hands. "I understand that this is not easy for you, Janelle," he said softly, "But Maria has been a part of my life for so long. We have a history together, and we share a bond."

Janelle felt her heart breaking as Tony continued to explain. He spoke of the years they had spent together, the challenges they had faced, and the deep connection they still shared. Tony stated that he had a sense of responsibility towards Maria, especially during these difficult times when she needed his support. He added that Maria had never been with another man, and that's why she still depends on him. While Janelle tried to comprehend Tony's words, she couldn't shake off the feeling of disappointment. She truly believed that the relationship between Tony and Maria had ended, but now she realized that they had just switched sides!! She was now in Maria's shoes!!

Tony held Janelle's emotionless body and said, "I love you, Janelle; I chose to be with you because you make me happy." At that moment, Janelle knew that Maria would be a permanent fixture in the relationship. Afraid of the answer Janelle whispered, "Are you sleeping with her?" Tony quietly replied Janelle, "Please don't ask me questions about what I do with my wife."